Born In Brooklyn

Journal

Christine Dunne

Christine Dunne, Publisher

Salinas, California 2020

ISBN-978-1-7350162-5-2

Printed by Lulu Press, Inc. in the United States of America.

First Printing, 2020

Christine Dunne, Publisher

P.O. Box 2002

Salinas, California 93902

www.deadland.co

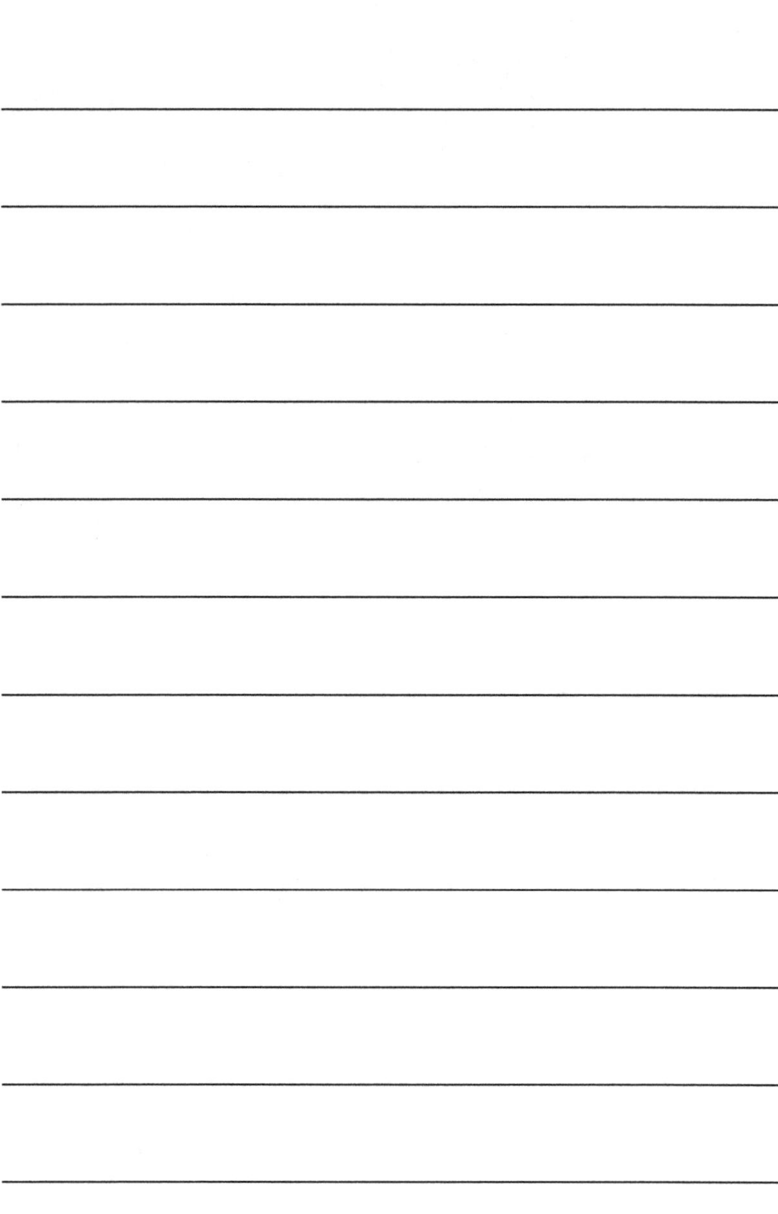

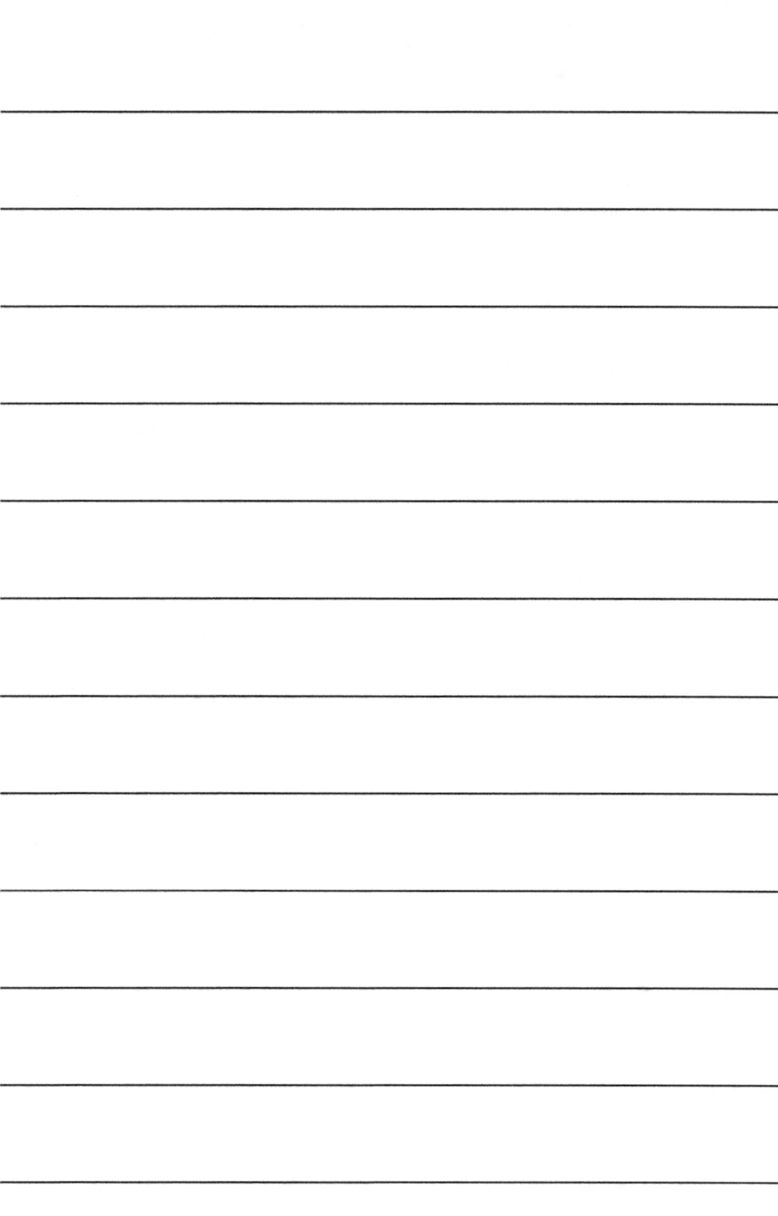

www.ingramcontent.com/pod-product-compliance
Lightning Source LLC
LaVergne TN
LVHW012331100826
845148LV00017B/2108

* 9 7 8 1 7 3 5 0 1 6 2 5 2 *